Does He Hear?

2nd Edition: Are You Ready?
The Discipleship Challenge

Martha A. Harper

ARCHWAY
PUBLISHING

Scripture taken from the Holy Bible, NEW INTERNATIONAL VERSION®. Copyright © 1973, 1978, 1984, 2011 by Biblica, Inc. All rights reserved worldwide. Used by permission. NEW INTERNATIONAL VERSION® and NIV® are registered trademarks of Biblica, Inc. Use of either trademark for the offering of goods or services requires the prior written consent of Biblica US, Inc.

Archway Publishing books may be ordered through booksellers or by contacting:

Archway Publishing
1663 Liberty Drive
Bloomington, IN 47403
www.archwaypublishing.com
1 (888) 242-5904

Because of the dynamic nature of the Internet, any web addresses or links contained in this book may have changed since publication and may no longer be valid. The views expressed in this work are solely those of the author and do not necessarily reflect the views of the publisher, and the publisher hereby disclaims any responsibility for them.

Any people depicted in stock imagery provided by Thinkstock are models, and such images are being used for illustrative purposes only. Certain stock imagery © Thinkstock.

ISBN: 978-1-4808-4100-0 (sc)
ISBN: 978-1-4808-4101-7 (e)

Library of Congress Control Number: 2016920349

Print information available on the last page.

Archway Publishing rev. date: 12/21/2016

Dedicated to

To the youth of our families and communities, who have expressed
their awareness of God and the knowledge that He is the answer
to all their questions, no matter what their age. They, each in
their own special way with deep emotions and heart desires,
are seeking God's help and direction through Jesus Christ and
the scriptures. I am impacted by their lives, the things they
have suffered and their search to know His will in their daily
lives. I pray you, the readers of this book, will find the God who
loves you and is there for you every minute of every day.

Ephesians 1:17

I keep asking that the God of our Lord Jesus Christ,
the glorious Father, may give you the Spirit of wisdom
and revelation, so that you may know him better.

Also written by Martha A. Harper

Does He Hear? (Life Devotions for Youth from Psalm 139)

Time to Eat! Christian devotional book for pre-school children

Contents

Foreword

I have much appreciation for Martha and this devotional guide. She has given much thought to the generations that will come behind her and offers easy to follow devotions intended to be used one day at a time. We are all very different and encounter so many different challenges, yet we still can relate to each other through God's Word. Many scenarios outlined may or may not have specifically happened to you, but there is a relatable element in each thought for the day. I applaud Martha for her desire to offer this spiritually minded material and you for seeking to read through it. As a youth minister for over a decade, I am convinced that the personal investment in material such as this book will be a great benefit to your walk with God.

Brad Poyet
Youth Minister - Argyle Church of Christ
Jacksonville, Florida

Preface

Interaction with several young people over an extended period of time sparked heart-felt questions which I had from my own youth, some continuing through my adult life. I wanted to reach out to communicate God's Word teaches us that He is listening. He wants to personally touch your lives. Whatever questions you have, whatever feelings are stirring within you regarding any circumstance in your life, God is there for you. Most of you have access to a significant amount of information through multiple avenues 24 hours a day, 7 days a week. Your parents also reserve the right to have daily input in your life. Then come your teachers in church and school. In addition, you are affected by the opinions of your peers (whether you admit it or not). This book is a start to introduce you to God, your creator and counselor, by looking at the questions, considering your feelings, and honestly sharing them with Him.

This 2nd edition, "Are You Ready? The Discipleship Challenge," is further encouragement to secure your personal relationship with God and claim Jesus Christ as Lord of your life in addition to recognizing Him as your Savior. The scriptures included offer you a challenge to explore the all-encompassing personal and practical aspects of an emerging and productive Christian life.

Acknowledgements

It is amazing how God uses different people and varied circumstances to move us along His directed path. From the beginning of my writing endeavor, the most productive times have been at the home of Ari and John, while sharing quiet moments on the river with Emma, their shepherd collie. Cindy graciously follows my ups and downs, prayerfully prodding me along through this journey. Doug and Betty continue to patiently listen and pray as I seek God's direction in my writing. Most recently Cyndi (a different one) perked my interest and accountability to finish this book. God has strategically moved her into a place in my life to encourage, pray, and keep me on track for timely publication and distribution.

For spiritual clarity and application, special thanks to:

Douglas Steele, Doctorates in Health Science & Physical Therapy; Former Assistant Professor of Allied Health, Harding University; Medical Missionary, Central and South America

Ownership

The questions in this book are not to rush through. God's Word is very serious and not just for adults. As you take time to read and ponder, you may want to use your own Bible for personal reading. You will find the concerns expressed are the same as people your age in other parts of the world. For each question and supporting scripture, there is an additional page with a question and space for your notes. Be honest with yourself and with God. What you write is between you and Him. Then pray to be strong and have the courage to follow His direction. Even as I write, I am praying for each of you who opens this book to open your heart to God who created you.

[** For Readers Only **]

A – The Secret Place

Question: God, when did you first know me?

Scripture: Psalm 139

vs. 15   My frame was not hidden from you when I was made in the secret place. When I was woven together in the depths of the earth,

vs. 16   your eyes saw my unformed body. All the days ordained for me were written in your book before one of them came to be.

Devotion: God has been aware of you from the beginning, even before you were born. He is eternal, and brought the world into being as He brought you into being. Nothing is hidden from God. He is the creator of all things and all people. We need to be assured that Jesus is our savior and takes care of all our wrongs and our sins. God is our creator who set us here to love Him, to love His world, and to be His children so He can love us.

Prayer: God, help me to understand who you are and how important I am to you. Thank you for caring about me. Even before I saw daylight or knew how to cry, you were taking care of me.

Your Time With God

Reader's Response to A

Find a quiet place, even outside under a tree if that is best.

After reading the first question, the scripture and the devotion, consider the additional question below. Ask God your questions and share your feelings. Write them out, also adding what you think God wants you to do about it.

When did I first become aware of God? What happened?

B – Were You There?

Question: God, what part did you play in creating me?

Scripture: Psalm 139

vs. 13   For you created my inmost being; you knit me together in my mother's womb.

vs. 14   I praise you because I am fearfully and wonderfully made; your works are wonderful, I know that full well.

Devotion: God is eternal and always present; He created you inside your mother, and He was there when you were born. Even if you had been born with an illness and something wrong with your physical body, God was there and ready to take care of you. Each child is created perfect in God's eyes, no matter what other people see. Some children are born and God decides to take them to be with Him right away. We may not understand why, but God is present and has a plan. If He kept you on earth, He has a purpose for you here.

Prayer: Help me, God, to understand that you see me as perfect. I am your creation and need to be sure of your love no matter what others may think.

Your Time with God

Reader's Response to B

Find a quiet place, maybe outside on your porch.

After reading the first question, the scripture and the devotion, consider the additional question below. Ask God your questions and share your feelings. Write them out, also adding what you think God wants you to do about it.

In what ways can you tell God is near you?

C – Who Cares?

Question: When I cried as a baby, someone usually picked me up. Now, if I cry into my pillow, who cares?

Scripture: Psalm 139

vs. 17   How precious to me are your thoughts, O God! How vast is the sum of them!

vs. 18   Were I to count them, they would outnumber the grains of sand. When I awake, I am still with you.

Devotion: If God created you, in addition to the whole universe, then clearly you are special to Him. You belong to Him, and He thinks about you all the time. Can you count the grains of sand in the desert or in a handful of sand on the beach? His thoughts about you are way more than the number of grains of sand. That is overwhelming to me. God does care all the time; we need to read His word, pray and be still to know His presence every hour of every day.

Prayer: God, I pray to receive your love, and to know how very special I am and how often you think about me. When I feel forgotten and like nobody cares, let me feel you near me. Let me see you in the things around me and feel your presence.

Your Time with God

Reader's Response to C

Find a quiet time and place, maybe early in the morning.

After reading the first question, the scripture and the devotion, consider the additional question below. Ask God your questions and share your feelings. Write them out, also adding what you think God wants you to do about it.

If Jesus always had a mom and dad here on earth
as well as a heavenly father, how could He ever
understand my hurt and being alone?

D – What Is Wrong With Me?

Question: My best friend doesn't want to hang out with me anymore. God, what is wrong with me?

Scripture: Psalm 139

vs. 15   My frame was not hidden from you when I was made in the secret place. When I was woven together in the depths of the earth,

vs. 16   your eyes saw my unformed body. All the days ordained for me were written in your book before one of them came to be.

Devotion: When you were made in secret, God knew your substance, even being imperfect. Every part of you was personally designed by the creator of the universe. You were fashioned by Him before any physical part was actually made. If you, or anyone else, sees something different or unpleasant, just remember that God sees you as His beautiful handiwork and loves every tiny part of you.

Prayer: God, help me to see myself and look at others the way you see me. I need to believe in your love and creation as the Word tells me. When I consider your opinion more important than others, I will be able to accept myself, love myself, and love others more.

Your Time with God

Reader's Response to D

Find a quiet place, maybe at school during lunch.

After reading the first question, the scripture and the devotion, consider the additional question below. Ask God your questions and share your feelings. Write them out, also adding what you think God wants you to do about it.

Is God truly the creator of all things? Do you trust Him for every part of your life - physically, emotionally, as well as spiritually?

E – Did You Know?

Question: I didn't get chosen for a team until the very last. I said some hurtful things, but no one heard me. God, did you know about this?

Scripture: Psalm 139

vs. 3 You discern my going out and my lying down; you are familiar with all my ways.

vs. 4 Before a word is on my tongue you know it completely, O Lord.

Devotion: Jesus knew rejection right from the start. He was born in secret, and His parents had to hide Him. As a man, His own people rejected Him and sent Him to die on the cross. Yes, He does understand and hears your angry words. He knows exactly how you feel. Have you ever thought about when someone else goes through the same rejection? Because you understand, maybe you could be an important part in helping them.

Prayer: God, I say I want to be more like Jesus, but I don't often think about the hurt and the suffering He went through. Help me to be strong like Him and think about helping someone else when they are hurting.

Your Time with God

Reader's Response to E

*Find a quiet place, ask permission to stay up
late to read and write before bedtime.*

*After reading the first question, the scripture and the
devotion, consider the additional question below. Ask God
your questions and share your feelings. Write them out, also
adding what you think God wants you to do about it.*

Does Jesus feel your hurt and rejection? Do you think He heard
your angry remarks even though you only said them to yourself?

F – Why Me?

Question: I want to hang out like my friends, but I have brothers and sisters to take care of. Why me?

Scripture: Psalm 139

vs. 1   O LORD, you have searched me and you know me.

vs. 2   You know when I sit and when I rise; you perceive my thoughts from afar.

vs. 3   You discern my going out and my lying down; you are familiar with all my ways.

Devotion: God knows your thoughts, emotions, and needs. He sees the sacrifices you make to take care of your brothers and sisters. Let Him know how you feel and ask Him to open your heart to serve Him more. Trust Him to give you time to be with your friends. The time may not be equal to others, but if you are doing God's work you will find peace and be happy, whatever He ask of you.

Prayer: I pray to understand your love for me and for each of my brothers and sisters. Help me to trust you to care for my needs and to reach out to help meet the needs of each of them.

Your Time with God

Reader's Response to F

Find a private place; try the back steps of your house.

After reading the first question, the scripture and the devotion, consider the additional question below. Ask God your questions and share your feelings. Write them out, also adding what you think God wants you to do about it.

Do you believe that God is as concerned about you as He is about your brothers and sisters? Can He meet the needs of all of you?

G – Is This Fair?

Question: Mom and Dad are getting a divorce. They want me to take sides and split my time between them. God, is this fair to me?

Scripture: Psalm 139

vs. 11   If I say, "Surely the darkness will hide me and the light become night around me,"

vs. 12   even the darkness will not be dark to you; the night will shine like the day, for darkness is as light to you.

Devotion: Sometimes circumstances seem so dark. You ask, what can I do? Is there a decision that is right for everybody? Your darkness is not dark to Him. He is light and will show you the way. You must 1) read His Word, 2) pray, telling Him your fears and your hurts, and 3) seek counsel from a Christian adult. God will provide assurance of His love, direction for what to do daily, and give you comfort. Put yourself in His care; wait and pray. You will find your path clearer.

Prayer: God, I know out of all the people in the world, you are aware of my troubles and care about Mom and Dad, too. As I read my Bible and pray, help me to trust you and to find your light in all of this.

Your Time with God

Reader's Response to G

*Find personal time and a quiet place, maybe
a nearby park or public library.*

*After reading the first question, the scripture and the
devotion, consider the additional question below. Ask God
your questions and share your feelings. Write them out, also
adding what you think God wants you to do about it.*

I'm the child in this situation. What can I do to find inner
peace for me and to help make a bad situation better?

H – Anyone looking?

Question: A boy who lives down the road rides his bike to school. He makes fun of me because I have to walk. I wanted to push him when no one was looking.

Scripture: Psalm 139

vs. 3   You discern my going out and my lying down; you are familiar with all my ways.

vs. 4   Before a word is on my tongue you know it completely, O LORD.

Devotion: God made you and knows what makes you mad or upset. He hears your thoughts and sees your actions when no one else does. He knows it hurts when people laugh at you. Remember God knows how you feel and will give you what you need, when you need it. He created you and knows what is best for you. Often what we want and what we need are two different things.

Prayer: God, help me to be grateful for being able to go to school. Also, I need to be thankful for how I get to school. Other students can't walk or have difficulty walking, taking more energy and time than I do. Help me deal with my "secret" sins.

Your Time with God

Readers Response to H

*Before you read, decide on a quiet place; think
before answering the question.*

*After reading the first question, the scripture and the
devotion, consider the additional question below. Ask God
your questions and share your feelings. Write them out, also
adding what you think God wants you to do about it.*

When someone makes fun of me, what can I do to control
how I feel? How do I respond to them as Jesus would?

I – Where Can I Hide?

Question: I've been doing some ugly things and going places which are not good for me. How do I stop hiding and find Jesus to make changes?

Scripture: Psalm 139

vs. 9   If I rise on the wings of the dawn, if I settle on the far side of the sea,

vs. 10   even there your hand will guide me, your right hand will hold me fast.

Devotion: God sees you no matter where you go or what you have done. If you want to change, He is ready to forgive you no matter what happened. Jesus died on the cross to forgive all your sins, was raised to life to be with God and take us with Him. Get a Bible to read His Word. Ask Him to send someone to encourage and advise you. If the first person you ask doesn't know how to help, keep praying. God will guide you to the right person.

Prayer: God, I've really messed up. Thank you for the forgiveness through Jesus, for waiting for me to come back and make things right. Show me where to go and the people I need to be around for daily help.

Your Time with God

Reader's Response to I

Be sure not to rush writing down your thoughts, most importantly be honest with yourself and God.

After reading the first question, the scripture and the devotion, consider the additional question below. Ask God your questions and share your feelings. Write them out, also adding what you think God wants you to do about it.

When I get dressed for each day do I ask God, 1) How do I look in my heart as well as on my face? and 2) Where will I go and will I take Jesus with me?

J – What Should I Do?

Question: I have a step-parent who uses a lot of bad language. They speak evil of you, God, and don't like me going to church. What should I do?

Scripture: Psalm 139

vs. 20   They speak of you with evil intent; your adversaries misuse your name.

vs. 24   See if there is any offensive way in me, and lead me in the way everlasting.

Devotion: There will always be people in your life who hate God. You may be afraid of them or find it hard to respect them. Be pure in your heart towards God no matter what someone else says. Forgive others and pray for them, trusting God to take care of their spiritual condition. Ask your pastor or Sunday school teacher to help work things out for your continued attendance at worship. And remember, you are to respect your parents and answer to God for your own words and actions.

Prayer: God, help me to control my temper and my words. Please get me help to stay in church. I pray to have the right attitude so what I do and say may help change someone else's heart.

Your Time with God

Reader's Response to J

*If you have more questions, write each down and
talk with someone close to you about them.*

*After reading the first question, the scripture and the
devotion, consider the additional question below. Ask God
your questions and share your feelings. Write them out, also
adding what you think God wants you to do about it.*

What things do I need to look at in my own heart to
change so people will see more of God in me?

K - Fewer Rules; More Freedom?

Question: My coach at school sometimes gives us privileges which my parents don't agree with. God, when I'm with him, I'm okay to do it his way, right?

Scripture: Psalm 139

vs. 2   You know when I sit and when I rise; you perceive my thoughts from afar.

vs. 3   You discern my going out and my lying down; you are familiar with all my ways.

Devotion: Obeying God's rules and respecting rules set by your parents is important. They protect us and guide us in every situation. The hard part is *not* doing what everyone else does, especially if we know it isn't right for us. Even if you are not caught, doing wrong things may really bother you. Sometimes once you've done something, it's easier to convince yourself that it's okay to do it again; and then things get worse. God's protection is secure when we come to Him and trust His care.

Prayer: Wow, God. You really are there for me all the time, day and night. Help me to listen to you, to read your Word, and make it a part of my daily thoughts to make better choices when it counts.

Your Time with God

Reader's Response to K

Don't rush. If you need to, put it down and come back
to it later. But don't wait too long to start again.

After reading the first question, the scripture and the
devotion, consider the additional question below. Ask God
your questions and share your feelings. Write them out, also
adding what you think God wants you to do about it.

What situations have I been in where I had the freedom to
make a choice and could have made a better one?

L – Where Were You, God?

Question: People broke into our home, and I was shot in the leg. I find I will lose part of my leg. Shouldn't those people be punished? Where were you, God, when this happened?

Scripture: Psalm 139

vs. 19   If only you would slay the wicked, O God! Away from me, you bloodthirsty men!

vs. 24   See if there is any offensive way in me, and lead me in the way everlasting.

Devotion: Some things happen which we don't understand. We are angry and confused. Trust God no matter what your circumstance; remember His primary protection for us is our souls. God will handle the evil people. We must forgive and not carry hate within us, destroying our connection with God. It affects relationships with families and friends. Be careful of the people you're around and pray for those who hurt you emotionally and physically.

Prayer: God, some things get really confusing. Help me trust you even if everything around me looks bad. Remind me to keep my heart open to you, and pray for those who need you.

Your Time with God

Reader's Response to L

*Quiet times are for you and God. Sometimes questions
are hard; ask an adult for help if you need it.*

*After reading the first question, the scripture and the
devotion, consider the additional question below. Ask God
your questions and share your feelings. Write them out, also
adding what you think God wants you to do about it.*

When did something happen to you that was unfair? Was it
fair when Jesus died on the cross for the sin in your life?

Epilogue

What have I learned?"

Reading your Bible, praying, and seeking trusted counsel will help you find answers and put them into practice. A relationship with God takes you one step at a time. May this book help you on your journey towards a challenging and rewarding relationship with your creator.

Are You Ready?

The Discipleship Challenge

Contents

Introduction

An opportunity was provided to publish a second edition of ***Does He Hear?*** Almost immediately and through prayer, I knew the direction God wanted me to take with this additional material. The first edition deals very specifically with your personal concepts of God through questions you might have. In this second edition, the original manuscript has been retained and the material, ***Are You Ready? The Discipleship Challenge,*** has been added. For review, the entire chapter of Psalm 139 is included. Study helps are provided as the book is interactive. An outline and more questions have been inserted to guide you through the Word to secure a personal relationship with Christ. It is important that you study your Bible, pray for God's direction, and make decisions for which you will be accountable to Him daily and for your lifetime.

Knowing Christ is not exclusive as your Savior. He is to be your **LORD and** Savior. As a disciple there are several things I would like to call to your attention. Change, commitment, clarity, and communication are relevant parts of 1) confessing our sin and repenting to change, 2) commitment to study and obey His Word, 3) clarity of truth daily in our minds, hearts and actions, and 4) communication with God in prayer, with other Christians, and with those who need Christ. These are just a few ... so let's get started.

Psalm 139

Vs. 1 O Lord, you have searched me and you know me. Vs. 2 You know when I sit and when I rise; you perceive my thoughts from afar. Vs. 3 You discern my going out and my lying down; you are familiar with all my ways. Vs. 4 Before a word is on my tongue you know it completely, O Lord. Vs. 5 You hem me in -- behind and before; you have laid your hand upon me. Vs. 6 Such knowledge is too wonderful for me, too lofty for me to attain. Vs. 7 Where can I go from your Spirit? Where can I flee from your presence? Vs. 8 If I go up to the heavens, you are there; if I make my bed in the depths, you are there. Vs. 9 If I rise on the wings of the dawn, if I settle on the far side of the sea, Vs. 10 even there your hand will guide me, your right hand will hold me fast. Vs. 11 If I say, "Surely the darkness will hide me and the light become night around me," Vs. 12 even the darkness will not be dark to you; the night will shine like the day, for darkness is as light to you. Vs. 13 For you created my inmost being; you knit me together in my mother's womb. Vs. 14 I praise you because I am fearfully and wonderfully made; your works are wonderful, I know that full well. Vs. 15 My frame was not hidden from you when I was made in the secret place. When I was woven together in the depths of the earth, Vs. 16 your eyes saw my unformed body. All the days ordained for me were written in your book before one of them came to be. Vs. 17 How precious to me are your thoughts, O God! How vast is the sum of them! Vs. 18 Were I to count them they would outnumber the grains of sand. When I awake, I am still with you. Vs. 19 If only you would slay the wicked, O God! Away from me, you bloodthirsty men! Vs. 20 They speak of you with evil intent; your adversaries misuse your name. Vs. 21 I have nothing but hatred for them; I count them my enemies. Vs. 23 Search me, O God, and know my heart; test me and know my anxious thoughts. Vs. 24 See if there is any offensive way in me and lead me in the way everlasting.

Personal Study Helps

A. Exploring His Word

❖ Read only one devotion per week.

❖ Read the devotion every day, first thing in the morning or just before you go to bed.

❖ Meditate on the Scripture.

❖ Write the Scripture on an index card or in a notebook.

❖ Carry it in your book bag, pocket or purse.

❖ Find a partner for sharing.

❖ Make a 12 week commitment to finish the devotions.

❖ Encourage one another with phone calls, texts, notes or e-mails.

❖ When one devotion is finished, review together and reward your attitude changes and personal growth.

(Personal Study Helps, continued)

B. **Exploring His Word**

1. A study Bible with commentary in the back and footnotes on each page

2. A church library or public library

3. A youth director at church

4. A teacher at school or university

5. Your parents, grandparents, aunt or uncle

6. A Christian book store (ask sales clerk for help)

7. A pastor or elder/deacon in your church

Personal Relationship with Jesus Christ

Who?   God, by His Word - 1 Peter 1: 23-25

What happened?   Creation - Genesis 1; Psalm 33: 6-9

Where are we?   Sin - Isaiah 55: 6, 7

Who is Christ?   Word is Jesus - John 1: 1 – 14; John 12: 47-50

When?   Confess our sin, accept Christ - Romans 3: 23, 24; Romans 6: 3-5

Why?   New life, reconciliation - 2 Corinthians 5: 17-19

REVIEW:

Where you are: In sin - Galatians 5: 19-21

Where you could be: Eternal peace - Galatians 5: 22-24

How to get there: Grace - Ephesians 1: 7, 8; Ephesians 2: 4-9

Why did He? Should I?   Deliver, transform - Colossians 1: 13-20

What happens?   Complete, forgiven - Colossians 2: 9–14

What happens, future?   Share, suffer, serve - 2 Timothy 2: 1-5

How to live and grow - 2 Timothy 2: 15-26; 2 Timothy 3: 16-17

What is the Christian Life About?

Character of God: Exodus 34: 5, 6 And he passed in front of Moses, proclaiming, "The Lord, the Lord, the compassionate and gracious God, slow to anger, abounding in love and faithfulness,

Profile of Jesus: Isaiah 9: 6, 7 For to us a child is born, to us a son is given, and the government will be on his shoulders. And he will be called Wonderful Counselor, Mighty God, Everlasting Father, Prince of Peace. Of the increase of his government and peace there will be no end. He will reign on David's throne and over his kingdom, establishing and upholding it with justice and righteousness from that time on and forever. The zeal of the Lord Almighty will accomplish this.

Holy Spirit: John 14:26 But the Counselor, the Holy Spirit, whom the Father will send in my name, will teach you all things and will remind you of everything I have said to you.

Being a Christian is not for the weak.

Count the Cost: Luke 14: 28 – 30 "Suppose one of you wants to build a tower. Will he not first sit down and estimate the cost to see if he has enough money to complete it? For if he lays the foundation and is not able to finish it, everyone who sees it will ridicule him, saying, "This fellow began to build and was not able to finish."

Popularity or Intelligence: Acts 4: 13 When they saw the courage of Peter and John and realized that they were unschooled, ordinary men, they were astonished and they took note that these men had been with Jesus.

Perseverance is crucial: Romans 5: 3 – 5 Not only so, we also rejoice in our sufferings, because we know that suffering produces perseverance; perseverance, character; and character, hope. And hope does not disappoint us, because God has poured out his love into our hearts by the Holy Spirit, whom he has given us.

Am I Ready to Commit?

> ➤ **Do I want to be a complete, whole person, fulfilled in Christ?**
> ➤ 2 Corinthians 5: 17-19 Therefore, if anyone is in Christ, he is a new creation; the old has gone, the new has come! All this is from God, who reconciled us to himself through Christ and gave us the ministry of reconciliation: that God was reconciling the world to himself in Christ, not counting men's sins against them. And he has committed to us the message of reconciliation.

> ➤ **How does change take place; by what power?**
> ➤ Colossians 1: 13-16 For he has rescued us from the dominion of darkness and brought us into the kingdom of the Son he loves, in whom we have redemption, the forgiveness of sins. He is the image of the invisible God, the firstborn over all creation. For by him all things were created in heaven and on earth, visible and invisible, whether thrones or powers or rulers or authorities; all things were created by him and for him.
> ➤ 1 Peter 3:21 and this water symbolizes baptism that now saves you also – not the removal of dirt from the body but the pledge of a good conscience toward God. It saves you by the resurrection of Jesus Christ,

Am I Ready to Commit? (continued)

- ➢ **Once changed, do I want to grow and mature?**
- ➢ 2 Timothy 3: 16, 17 All Scripture is God-breathed and is useful for teaching, rebuking, correcting and training in righteousness, so that the man of God may be thoroughly equipped for every good work.

- ➢ **Even as a Christian, I am not perfect. I may still sin. What am I to do then?**
- ➢ Hebrews 4: 15, 16 For we do not have a high priest who is unable to sympathize with our weaknesses, but we have one who has been tempted in every way, just as we are – yet was without sin. Let us then approach the throne of grace with confidence so that we may receive mercy and find grace to help us in our time of need.

- ➢ **If I am on God's path, what could interfere?**
- ➢ 1 John 2:15 – 17 Do not love the world or anything in the world. If anyone loves the world, the love of the Father is not in him. For everything in the world – the cravings of sinful man, the lust of his eyes and the boasting of what he has and does – comes not from the Father but from the world. The world and its desires pass away, but the man who does the will of God lives forever.

Christianity is Living and Active ...

Psalm 1: 1 – 3 Blessed is the man who does not walk in the counsel of the wicked or stand in the way of sinners or sit in the seat of mockers. But his delight is in the law of the Lord, and on his law he meditates day and night. He is like a tree planted by streams of water which yields its fruit in season and whose leaf does not wither. Whatever he does prospers.
Note: There is a progression of action. First the man was walking, listening to wicked people around him. Then he stopped, standing with them and thinking their thoughts. Then he was sitting and actively became a part of them.

Isaiah 55: 8 – 11 For my thoughts are not your thoughts, neither are your ways my ways, declares the Lord. As the heavens are higher than the earth, so are my ways higher than your ways and my thoughts than your thoughts. As the rain and the snow come down from heaven, and do not return to it without watering the earth and making it bud and flourish, so that it yields seed for the sower and bread for the eater, so is my word that goes out from my mouth: It will not return to me empty, but will accomplish what I desire and achieve the purpose for which I sent it.
Note: Remember it is not what we say that promises results, but what God says through His Word. Know God's Word. Take every opportunity to share scripture with others, then watch God work!

How It All Starts ...

2 Peter 1: 22 – 25 Now that you have purified yourselves by obeying the truth so that you have sincere love for your brothers, love one another deeply, from the heart. For you have been born again, not of perishable seed, but of imperishable, through the living and enduring word of God. For, "All men are like grass, and all their glory is like the flowers of the field; the grass withers and the flowers fall, but the word of the Lord stands forever." And this is the word that was preached to you.

Are You Ready?

There are times you feel God is far away, removed from what is happening to you. You may surround yourself with noise so you do not always hear, but nonetheless God is available. You hear Him readily in nature. The birds sing, the sea roars, and trees rustle in the wind. They speak of God's power and wonder, and you hear Him saying, "I am right here; you are not abandoned."

God speaks in Scripture with a certain and specific message to us. These are not dust covered words meant only for ancient people long dead. The words are living and active. They connect with us, making us aware of God's presence. Slow down, turn off the noise for the moment, and listen to God. Seek a quiet place, an isolated corner to listen intently. Hearing God is a long term project. You are accustomed to fast, instant results. I remember a situation in the gospels. Jesus started to wash the feet of His friends, a task usually performed by the lowest of servants. One of the friends questioned what was happening. Jesus replied, "You do not realize now what I am doing, but later you will understand." Be patient and go the distance with God. Listen for Him. You will eventually realize what God is doing, and it will be marvelous!

Read a few lines of God's Word, repeat it two or three times. Close your eyes to see what stays with you, a word, a phrase, a picture - you will begin to sense God is leaving impressions with you. These are not just warnings to the historical King David or a command for Moses from a burning bush; they become a message for you. So read, ask, follow the devotion, and write. Be sure to write. At some point you can return to what you have written and mark your growth, tracing the path to the place God has brought you.

Guard your time with Him, no phone beeps, no message alerts, no ear buds. Listen to Him, then He wants to hear from you. Conversation builds a relationship. Don't rush it. Don't make it mechanical. He's listening for your heart and its openness to Him. Continue the path you have begun. And when God ask, "Do you hear Me?" then answer "I can," because you have chosen to, training yourself to turn down the noise of the world and listen to the creator of the universe. And He will dwell with you, refreshing your spirit and renewing your heart. God bless!

Ken Mick, **Living by the grace and blood of Jesus Christ,**
Growing by the power and wisdom of God's Word,
Serving by guidance of the Holy Spirit in His Word.

Printed in the United States
By Bookmasters